NEYMAR

NEYMAR

Odysseys

AIDAN WHITCOMB

CREATIVE EDUCATION · CREATIVE PAPERBACKS

Published by Creative Education and Creative Paperbacks
P.O. Box 227, Mankato, Minnesota 56002
Creative Education and Creative Paperbacks are imprints of
The Creative Company
www.thecreativecompany.us

Design by Tom Morgan
Art direction by Blue Design (www.bluedes.com)

Images by Associated Press/David Niviere/Abaca Press, cover, 59; Dreamstime/Andre Ricardo Paes, 60, 72, MaxiSports, 4–5, 34–35, Stefan Ugljevarevic, 63; Getty Images/Christian Liewig, 39, Cui Nan/China News Service, 8, Hector Vivas - FIFA, 11, JEWEL SAMAD, 56, Khalil Bashar/Jam Media, 64, Michael Regan - UEFA, 54–55, NELSON ALMEIDA, 75, Soccrates Images, 6, Tim Clayton, 20, Urbanandsport/NurPhoto, 49; Wikimedia Commons/Agência Brasil, 2, Alex Fau, 28, Antoine Dellenbach, 46, 69, Balkan Photos, 50, Christopher Johnson, 26, Danilo Borges/Portal da Copa, 24, 33, Fernando Frazão/Agência Brasil, 40, 43, Jimmy Baikovicius, 12, Ronnie Macdonald, 16, 19

Every effort has been made to contact copyright holders for material reproduced in this book. Any omissions will be rectified in subsequent printings if notice is given to the publisher.

Copyright © 2026 Creative Education, Creative Paperbacks
International copyright reserved in all countries. No part of this book may be reproduced in any form without written permission from the publisher.

Library of Congress Cataloging-in-Publication Data
Names: Whitcomb, Aidan author
Title: Neymar / by Aidan Whitcomb.
Description: Mankato, Minnesota : Creative Education and Creative Paperbacks, [2026] | Series: Odysseys in sports. Soccer stars | Includes bibliographical references and index. | Audience: Ages 12-15 | Audience: Grades 7-9 | Summary: "Neymar dazzled soccer fans at Santos, Barcelona, and PSG, and became Brazil's all-time top goal scorer. This action-packed biography for early high schoolers kicks up interest in his exceptional career"– Provided by publisher.
Identifiers: LCCN 2025012509 (print) | LCCN 2025012510 (ebook) | ISBN 9798895811412 library binding | ISBN 9798896800941 paperback | ISBN 9798895812679 ebook
Subjects: LCSH: Neymar, 1992- | Soccer midfielders–Brazil–Biography–Juvenile literature | Soccer players–Brazil–Biography–Juvenile literature
Classification: LCC GV942.7.N455 W45 2026 (print) | LCC GV942.7.N455 (ebook) | DDC 796.334092 [B]-dc23/eng/20250603
LC record available at https://lccn.loc.gov/2025012509
LC ebook record available at https://lccn.loc.gov/2025012510
Classification: LCC GV942.7.V56 W55 2026 (print) | LCC GV942.7.V56 (ebook) | DDC 796.334092 [B]-dc23/eng/20250603
LC record available at https://lccn.loc.gov/2025012511
LC ebook record available at https://lccn.loc.gov/2025012512

Printed in the United States

Neymar is one of the best players of the 21st century.

CONTENTS

Introduction 9

A Budding Star in Brazil 13

Attention in the Academy 20

Global Recognition 26

Reaching New Heights in Spain 29

'La Remontada' 35

Champions League History 39

A Golden Moment 43

A Fresh Start in France 44

PSG's First Charge 54

A Flopping Problem? 56

Injury Issues Mount 61

Messi Takes the Glory Once More 75

Selected Bibliography 76

Glossary 77

Websites 79

Index 80

Introduction

It's deep into extra time of a scoreless stalemate in the 2022 Qatar **FIFA** World Cup quarterfinals. Yellow Brazilian jerseys and red-and-white checkered Croatia kits fill Education City Stadium. Neymar, leading Brazil, receives the ball 30 yards from goal and plans his attack. He plays the ball into Rodrygo, who gives it right back. At the edge of the penalty area, Neymar slips it into the feet

OPPOSITE: Neymar scores the first goal for Brazil during the 2022 World Cup quarterfinal match against Croatia.

of Lucas Paquetá. Paquetá slickly slides the ball back to Neymar, just yards from goal. Each touch is precise and controlled. The onrushing Croatian keeper lunges toward Neymar's feet, but the attacker shifts out to the right. The goal opens for only a moment. Neymar blasts the ball into the roof of the net, and Brazilian fans erupt in celebration. Croatian defenders are stunned. In a moment of genius, Neymar ties the legendary Pelé as Brazil's all-time leading scorer.

When people think of the 21st century's greatest soccer players, Lionel Messi and Cristiano Ronaldo are usually the first two to come to mind. But, maybe the generation's third greatest is the Brazilian boy who went from being a prolific prospect in his home nation to being a key contributor in some of the greatest attacking trios in history.

Neymar celebrates after scoring for Brazil during the 2022 World Cup in Qatar.

A Budding Star in Brazil

Neymar da Silva Santos Júnior was born on February 5, 1992, in Mogi das Cruzes, São Paulo, Brazil. As the son of a professional soccer player, Neymar admired his father and wanted to follow in his footsteps. As Neymar grew up in Brazil, **futsal** played a large role in his development. Futsal helped develop his dribbling, control, and quick decision making. From a young age, Neymar set himself apart from other talents.

OPPOSITE: Neymar in a Santos FC jersey

In 1999, Neymar joined the Portuguesa Santista youth club. Quickly, larger clubs began to take notice. At age 11, Neymar caught the eye of one of Brazil's largest clubs, Santos FC. Santos FC's storied youth academy has produced many legends. One of soccer's greatest came through Santos nearly 50 years before Neymar: "O Rei" ("The King"), Pelé.

Neymar quickly shot up the youth system. He dazzled against other young players in the academy. He was ready for the next step. On March 7, 2009, he was awarded a debut with Santos. The 17-year-old was subbed on for the end of a league match in a 2–1 win against Oeste. It was a proud moment for Neymar and his family. A week later, Neymar scored his first professional goal against Mogi Mirim. The youngster began to settle in. His technical ability and flair were unmatched. Neymar drew the eyes of the nation to Santos matches and was a key contributor to the team throughout the season. In the 2009 **Campeonato Paulista** semifinal, Neymar scored the winning goal in a 2–1 victory against Brazilian giant Palmeiras. Although the team fell in the final against Corinthians, Neymar's first season was a success. He finished second on the team in goals, scoring 14 times in 48 appearances.

Heading into his second year and first full season as a professional, Neymar was poised to make an even bigger splash for the team. Santos also looked to cash in on the opportunity and build a team around their superstar. The club brought in several highly touted players such as Ganso, Wesley, and Robinho. The 2010 season marked a turning of the tide for Santos. Neymar scored 17 goals in 19 appearances in the Campeonato Paulista

Neymar made his debut for Brazil in 2010.

en route to an 18th championship. Neymar scored twice in the finals against Santo André. He was awarded the competition's best player award. Santos also won their first **Copa do Brasil** title.

Neymar finished 2010 with an impressive 42 goals in 60 appearances. Many Brazilians thought the 2010 World Cup could be the perfect opportunity to launch Neymar's national team career. However, the inexperienced Neymar wasn't included in the squad. Post-World Cup, Neymar did receive his first international call-up. He made his debut against the United States. In just 28 minutes, Neymar powered home a header past U.S. goalkeeper Tim Howard. Neymar finished third in the 2010 South American Footballer of the Year award. European clubs opened their checkbooks for him. West

Ham and Chelsea made bids. But Santos, and Neymar, remained firm. He was to stay in Brazil.

The player and the club had another successful season in 2011. Fans flocked to Santos matches to watch the youngster. The season was also Neymar's first **Copa Libertadores** experience. Santos entered the tournament with title hopes. They hadn't won since Pelé led them to back-to-back victories in 1962 and 1963. Santos turned around a tough start, winning their final three group stage matches. In the knockouts, Neymar and Santos were on fire. Santos made it to the final against Uruguay's premier club Peñarol. In the final, Neymar delivered. After a tight 0–0 first **leg** draw, he scored the opener in the second and carried the team to a 2–1 victory. Neymar gave Santos their first Copa Libertadores since Pelé. Neymar became

Neymar was key to Santos FC's success in 2011.

Attention in the Academy

In the Santos Academy, Neymar honed his skills. He became known for his amazing combination of speed, agility, and creativity. As Santos fans learned more about the teenage sensation, word began to spread. At age 14, Neymar was already being scouted by European clubs. Neymar even traveled to Spain to try out with Real Madrid's youth team. Santos were keen to keep their prodigy, and Neymar was keen to stay. He felt most comfortable in Brazil. He believed Santos gave him the best opportunity to develop. With the help of an enticing contract, Neymar decided to spend his formative years with Santos.

one of the youngest players to win the South American Footballer of the Year award at 19.

Neymar entered 2012 as soccer's biggest young star. The year was full of achievements. In a feisty February match against Palmeiras, Neymar tallied his 100th professional goal on his 20th birthday. In May, he became the highest scorer, since Pelé, in Santos history. Santos won their third straight Campeonato Paulista title. Neymar led the competition with 20 goals in 16 games. In the final against Guaraní, he scored four great goals over the two legs. He unquestionably remained the league's best player.

Neymar also had the first opportunity to play for his country at a major tournament. He was a key member of the Brazilian 2012 Olympic squad. He dominated the group stage, tallying two goals and two assists. Brazil navigated through the knockouts past Honduras and

South Korea before matching up against Mexico for the gold medal. However, Neymar fell short and had to settle for silver. Putting a bow on the year, Neymar again was named South American Footballer of the Year. Neymar grew into an even more versatile player. His ability to attack from all angles gave defenders nightmares.

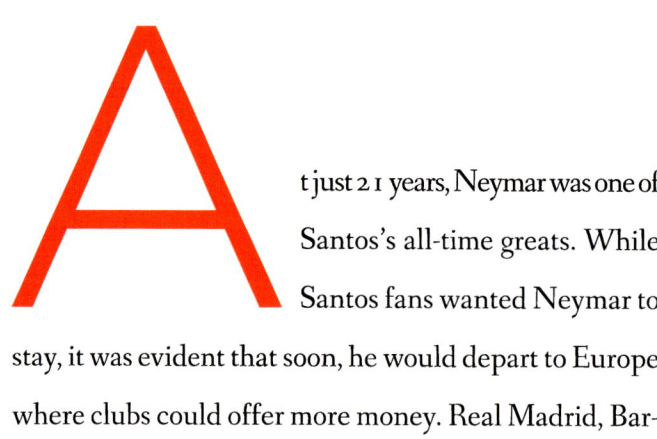

At just 21 years, Neymar was one of Santos's all-time greats. While Santos fans wanted Neymar to stay, it was evident that soon, he would depart to Europe where clubs could offer more money. Real Madrid, Barcelona, and Chelsea showed great interest in Neymar, even as his price skyrocketed. His days in Brazil were numbered. Regardless, Neymar vowed to finish on a high.

Once again, he excelled in the Paulista, scoring twice in the opening match. He bagged four goals against Uniao Barbarense in April. He led the team with 12 goals in 18 appearances. Toward the end of the season, Neymar revealed his intent to leave for Europe in May. It was an emotional day for Neymar and *Peixe* (another name for Santos) fans alike.

On May 24, 2013, Santos announced that two offers had been placed on Neymar. The next day, Neymar made his decision. He would join Spanish club Barcelona. He followed in the footsteps of many Brazilian stars before him including Ronaldinho, Rivaldo, and Romário. Neymar cried

Neymar plays for Brazil in the 2013 FIFA Confederations Cup final against Spain.

as the national anthem played prior to his final Santos match against Flamengo. He left Santos with 136 goals, having delivered three Paulistas, a Libertadores, and a Copa do Brasil. One of the brightest eras in Santos history closed.

eymar's **transfer fee** was an expensive $74 million. The 21-year-old signed a five-year deal with Barcelona and was showcased at Barcelona stadium Camp Nou before 56,500 fans. Pairing Neymar with superstars like Lionel Messi and Andres Iniesta, Barcelona looked to be one of Europe's best, with aspirations beyond **La Liga**.

Global Recognition

Because of their success in the 2011 Libertadores, Santos qualified for the 2011 FIFA Club World Cup. Representing South America, Neymar continued to impress. He scored a stunning strike from distance against Japanese club Kashiwa Reysol in the semifinal. In the final, Santos faced the kings of Europe, Barcelona. Despite Neymar's efforts, the Spanish club routed the Brazilians 4-0. Neymar received the 2011 FIFA Puskas Award, given to the player who scores the best goal in the world that year. His mesmerizing solo effort against Flamengo, dribbling through a multitude of hapless defenders, granted him the honor.

Before joining Barcelona, Neymar was selected by Brazil for the 2013 FIFA Confederations Cup. Neymar wanted to excite fans on home soil before the 2014 World Cup. In the tournament's opener, he got the party started three minutes in with a goal against Japan. Neymar received the ball off the chest of teammate Fred and lashed a stunning volley into the top right corner. Neymar also scored against Mexico and Italy in the last two group matches. Brazil got past Uruguay in the semifinals to face defending World Cup champion Spain. Spain had won 29 straight games, but Neymar put an end to the Spaniards', and some future teammates', run. He assisted the opener and powered a left-footed rocket past Spanish goalkeeper Iker Casillas for the Brazilians' second goal en route to a commanding 3–0 victory.

Reaching New Heights in Spain

Full of confidence, Neymar headed to Barcelona with the goal of instantly becoming a focal point of the club's attack. On August 18, 2013, Neymar made his debut against Levante. Three days later, he scored his first competitive goal for his new club against Atletico Madrid. While Neymar was an important player for coach

OPPOSITE: Neymar made his debut for storied Spanish club Barcelona in 2013.

Tata Martino's team, he had some early difficulties adjusting to the grueling style of European soccer. He was undersized in Europe, and defenders were much more skilled than those he faced in Brazil. He had to work for minutes in a stacked squad that included Messi, Pedro, and Alexis Sánchez. Still, Neymar pushed hard and had some massive performances in his initial season.

In La Liga, Neymar blended goals with creativity, scoring 9 and assisting 10 in 26 games. One of the most memorable moments occurred in his first **El Clásico**, an October match at the Camp Nou. Neymar scored the opener, cutting in on his right foot to roll the ball past the Real Madrid keeper. Neymar also assisted Sánchez's audacious chip for the second goal in a 2–1 triumph. As Neymar was subbed off, he received enormous applause from the nearly 100,000 Barcelona faithful. While Neymar often played second fiddle to Messi, he still racked up 15 goals across all competitions. He was developing chemistry with one of the all-time greats.

After the La Liga season, the 22-year-old faced some of the most intense pressure of his young career. He traveled home to take part in the 2014 World Cup. Coming off Brazil's success in the Confederations Cup, there were high expectations. With the world's eyes turned to São Paulo for the opener, Neymar had a fantastic performance. Neymar tied the game in the first half and scored what proved to be the winner with a second-half penalty kick. He was named Man of the Match. In the final group-stage game, he again scored twice in a 4–1 defeat of Cameroon. A thrilling round-of-16 battle with Chile went to penalty kicks. Neymar held his composure, burying the winning kick. Next came Colombia, and Neymar assisted Thiago Silva's opener. Brazil looked dominant. Then, tragedy struck. Late in the match, Neymar collided with a defender and hit the ground. The stadium fell silent. A fractured vertebra ended Neymar's magical run. As he left the field in tears, the energy in the Brazilian team dropped. Although they advanced past Colombia, they ran into Germany in the semifinals. Without Neymar, Brazil was humiliated, losing 1–7. Despite Neymar coming up short, the tournament cemented his status as a national hero. Neymar shined on soccer's biggest stage.

After the World Cup, Neymar reached new heights in 2014–15, flourishing into one of the greatest players in the world. With Messi and new signing Luis Suárez, Neymar became part of the trio known as "MSN." The

Defenders guard Neymar closely.

MSN trio would lead Barcelona through a historic season. In La Liga, Neymar scored 22 goals and provided 7 assists. Barcelona battled with Real Madrid, with the season coming down to the final day. Neymar assisted Messi in a 2–2 draw with Deportivio La Coruna, clinching the title over runners-up Real Madrid.

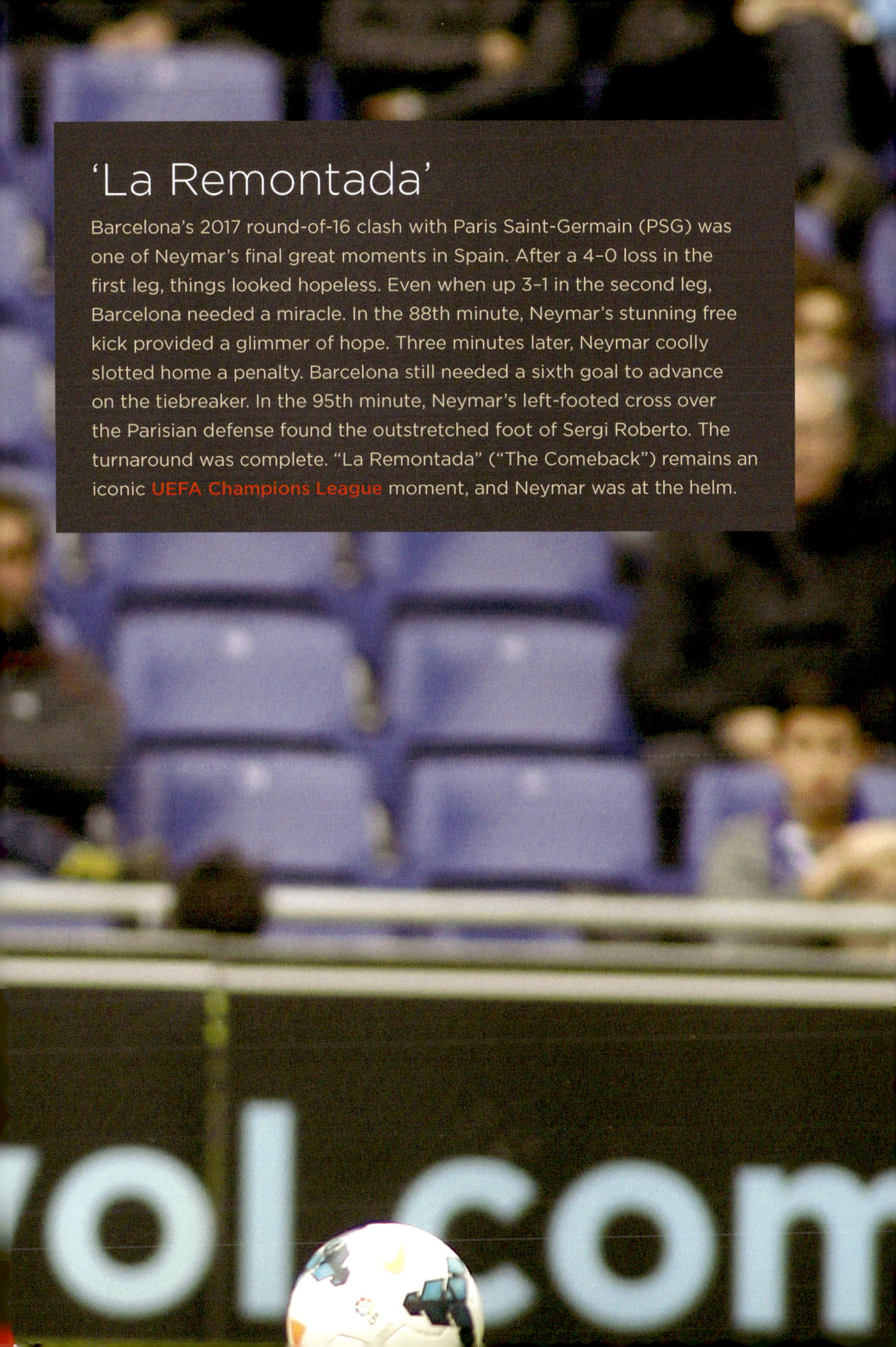

'La Remontada'

Barcelona's 2017 round-of-16 clash with Paris Saint-Germain (PSG) was one of Neymar's final great moments in Spain. After a 4-0 loss in the first leg, things looked hopeless. Even when up 3-1 in the second leg, Barcelona needed a miracle. In the 88th minute, Neymar's stunning free kick provided a glimmer of hope. Three minutes later, Neymar coolly slotted home a penalty. Barcelona still needed a sixth goal to advance on the tiebreaker. In the 95th minute, Neymar's left-footed cross over the Parisian defense found the outstretched foot of Sergi Roberto. The turnaround was complete. "La Remontada" ("The Comeback") remains an iconic UEFA Champions League moment, and Neymar was at the helm.

Across all competitions, Neymar netted 39 goals and was named in the UEFA Team of the Year. Neymar also finished third in the 2015 **Ballon d'Or**. The MSN trio broke all kinds of scoring records and helped Barcelona win the Champions League, along with the Copa del Rey and La Liga, completing the **treble**. Barcelona soccer was beautiful to watch, and the front three devastated opponents.

The international season was also an important time for Neymar. Brazilian manager Dunga named Neymar captain of the national team. He also faced a bit of controversy. In a heated match against Colombia in the 2015 Copa América, Neymar was red carded for intentionally booting the ball at a Colombian player after the final whistle. He was suspended for the rest of the tournament.

The following La Liga season marked the peak of the MSN era. Neymar piled up 24 goals and 12 assists in league play. His best display came against Rayo Vallecano in October when he scored four times in a 5–2 victory. His assist for the fifth goal might have been the best, as he lifted a perfectly weighted cross over the defense onto the waiting foot of Suárez. Barcelona repeated as La Liga champions by a single point. Neymar also scored a game-sealing goal in extra time of a wild Copa del Rey final against Sevilla. Barcelona found success in the FIFA Club World Cup, too. After finishing as runner-up with Santos years before, Neymar lifted the trophy in 2015.

Over the course of the season, Neymar scored 31 times. Combined with Messi's 41 goals and Suárez's unbelievable 59, MSN rewrote the goal-scoring record books.

In 2016, Rio de Janeiro, Brazil, hosted the Olympics. Neymar believed this could be the perfect chance to claim the first-ever Olympic soccer gold for his country. Things weren't easy to start. Back-to-back scoreless draws against South Africa and Iraq frustrated the star and fans. Brazil was in jeopardy of not even escaping the group. Brazil managed to advance after beating Denmark, but Neymar was yet to score or assist.

Champions League History

Neymar's 2014–15 Champions League run was historic for many reasons. He finished as the competition's joint top scorer with 10 goals, including a stunning 7 in the knockouts. His best performance came against Paris Saint-Germain in the quarterfinals, when he scored once in the away leg and twice at home to advance. In the final against Juventus, Neymar put the cherry on top of a ruthless Barcelona performance, scoring the third in a 3–1 victory. In doing so, Neymar became the first player since 1992 to score in each leg of a Champions League season from the quarterfinals on.

2016 Olympics

Finally, in the knockout stages, Neymar came alive. In the quarterfinals, Neymar curled home a long-range free kick against Colombia. He followed with a pair of goals in a 6–0 beatdown of Honduras. In the final against Germany, Neymar had his best Brazilian moment. After a great goal in regular time, Neymar scored the winning goal in a penalty shootout in front of his own country.

This triumph was a major turning point in his career. Neymar was blossoming into a natural leader, capable of handling even the most immense pressure.

    Coming off a historic summer, Neymar was poised to excel. In July, he signed a five-year contract extension. It appeared that he wanted to continue with Barcelona through his prime. In the league, Neymar scored 13 goals and provided 11 assists. He remained a key part of the engine that made Barcelona go but often saw less praise than his counterparts Messi and Suárez. In the Champions League, Neymar had his best performance against Celtic. In a 7–0 victory, he served up four assists and added a free-kick goal for good measure. He also scored twice and assisted in the round-of-16 win against Paris Saint-Germain. Ultimately, Neymar completed his 2016–17 campaign with 20 goals and 21 assists.

One of the most shocking moments came after the season. In July 2017, the media got wind of a possible transfer rumor. PSG came calling. As he had signed a large contract with Barcelona, many thought the rumor was just that, a rumor. But Neymar desired something different—a chance to step out of the shadow of Messi. It was a difficult decision, but on August 2, Neymar asked Barcelona to sell him. A day later, it was announced that Neymar would be sold to PSG for a whopping $258 million. Neymar became the most expensive transfer of all time.

In 186 career matches with Barcelona, Neymar recorded 105 goals, becoming one of 20 players ever to score 100-plus goals for the club. A magnificent era had come to a close, but the chance to become the "Prince of Paris" awaited.

A Golden Moment

The 2016 Olympic gold medal match was one of Neymar's finest performances. Ironically, it came against Germany who had embarrassed Brazil two summers earlier. Neymar's goal in regular time was sensational. His looping free kick off the crossbar sent the Brazilian stadium into chaos. Germany equalized, but the ensuing penalty kick shootout provided one of Neymar's most emotional moments. Both sides scored their first four kicks, but Brazilian goalkeeper Weverton got low to save the Germans' fifth. Up stepped Neymar with a chance for glory—a golden chance. Neymar gave the ball a kiss, placed it on the spot, and calmly converted. He dropped to his knees in tears as his teammates celebrated with him.

A Fresh Start in France

Despite the likes of Messi and Suárez playing in Barcelona, the PSG attack was plenty lethal. Fellow South Americans Edinson Cavani and Ángel Di María had plenty of experience. A rising star transferred in from Monaco named Kylian Mbappé also excited fans. Neymar made his dazzling PSG debut against Guingamp on

August 13, 2017, scoring once and assisting another time. He tallied twice more against Toulouse a week later in front of 47,000 home fans. The 2017–18 Champions League campaign also started fast, with Neymar scoring in the first two group games. He was rapidly settling in and spearheading a lethal attacking core. It drew comparisons to the one he had left a few months earlier. In recognition for his fantastic 2017 year, Neymar equaled his best finish in the Ballon d'Or, finishing third, behind Messi and Ronaldo.

Neymar and PSG began to dream of the new heights they could reach. Early into the new season, PSG had nearly wrapped up the **Ligue 1** title and clinched a spot in the **Coupe de la Ligue** final. With a top of the table finish in their Champions League group, a big haul of trophies was expected.

2016 Olympics

However, a major wrench was thrown into the works. It started with a crushing 3–1 first leg defeat by Real Madrid in the round of 16 of the Champions League. Then, weeks later, Neymar suffered a serious metatarsal fracture injury. Surgery was required, and Neymar's fantastic debut season came to an abrupt end.

Without Neymar, PSG didn't look nearly as sharp. They would win the league title and a pair of domestic tournaments. They weren't able to mount a comeback against Real Madrid.

At the end of his first season in Paris, Neymar finished with a remarkable 28 goals and 16 assists in just 30 appearances. He was even named Ligue 1 Player of the Year. He had truly become the star of the show in Paris and had emerged from whatever shadow he was in at Barcelona. Although the transfer fee was incredibly high, PSG were encouraged with his initial output.

Rushing back from foot surgery, Neymar looked to achieve something he hadn't yet done—win a World Cup. Neymar wanted desperately to avenge the humiliation

OPPOSITE Messi and Neymar celebrate during a Champions League match between Barcelona and PSG in 2017.

suffered in the previous edition. Before Brazil's first match, it was not certain Neymar would be fit to play. But he was included in the starting lineup against Switzerland. The Swiss had a strategy for containing Neymar. Many teams would copy it throughout the remainder of his career: using physicality. Neymar was fouled 10 times in the Switzerland match and largely held in check. Being cautious with his foot injury, Neymar wasn't as effective as he would have wished. The game ended in a 1–1 draw. In the second match, Neymar again was hushed for 90-plus minutes by Costa Rica. Finally, the team broke through in added time, with Neymar scoring the second goal, tapping home a cross to seal the win. With a 2–0 win over Serbia, Brazil advanced to the round of 16. Against Mexico, Neymar delivered his signature performance of the tournament, scoring a

Neymar in 2018

goal and setting up Roberto Firmino for the second. Yet, in the biggest matchup of the quarterfinals, Brazil was stopped by Belgium. Neymar and Brazil would have to wait another four years to try again.

Back in Paris, Neymar's 2018–19 season was once again disrupted by injuries. Expectations were high for PSG, but while they dominated in France, they struggled in Europe, especially when without their star. Neymar only managed 17 Ligue 1 appearances out of a possible 34. Despite goals in the first four games of the season, all his stats dropped considerably as he missed significant time. In the Champions League, Neymar scored a brilliant hat trick against Red Star Belgrade. But in January 2019, Neymar re-aggravated the foot injury he had suffered the previous season. The injury held him out of a round-of-16 match with Manchester

United, in which PSG squandered a two-goal first-leg advantage. Neymar watched in frustration, taking to social media after the game to criticize the officials. As a result, he was suspended for three matches in the next year's competition.

In total, Neymar missed three months at a crucial point of the PSG season. Across all competitions, Neymar scored 23 times in 28 games. When he was on the field, there was no denying his ability. But he was simply too often unavailable. In the summer of 2019, Neymar was again injured in an international **friendly**, forcing him to miss the 2019 Copa América. Rumors also circulated that Neymar wished for a move back to Barcelona. However, PSG dismissed the rumors, and Neymar continued in Paris for the 2019–20 season.

More injury issues persisted in the following season, but Neymar also led PSG on their first charge at the Champions League title. In the league, Neymar was limited to only 15 appearances. He did score 13 times, including a fantastic 92nd-minute winner against Strasbourg in September. Receiving a sweeping left-footed cross from Abdou Diallo, Neymar scored a beautiful left-footed bicycle kick, clinching the victory. He missed nearly all of November with a hamstring injury but made key contributions on his return.

Then, the COVID-19 pandemic put soccer on pause. But Neymar played some of his best soccer once the world was ready to resume. On July 24, 2020, more than four and a half months after the semifinals, Neymar scored the only goal in a **Coupe de France** finals victory over Saint-Étienne. But the Champions League is

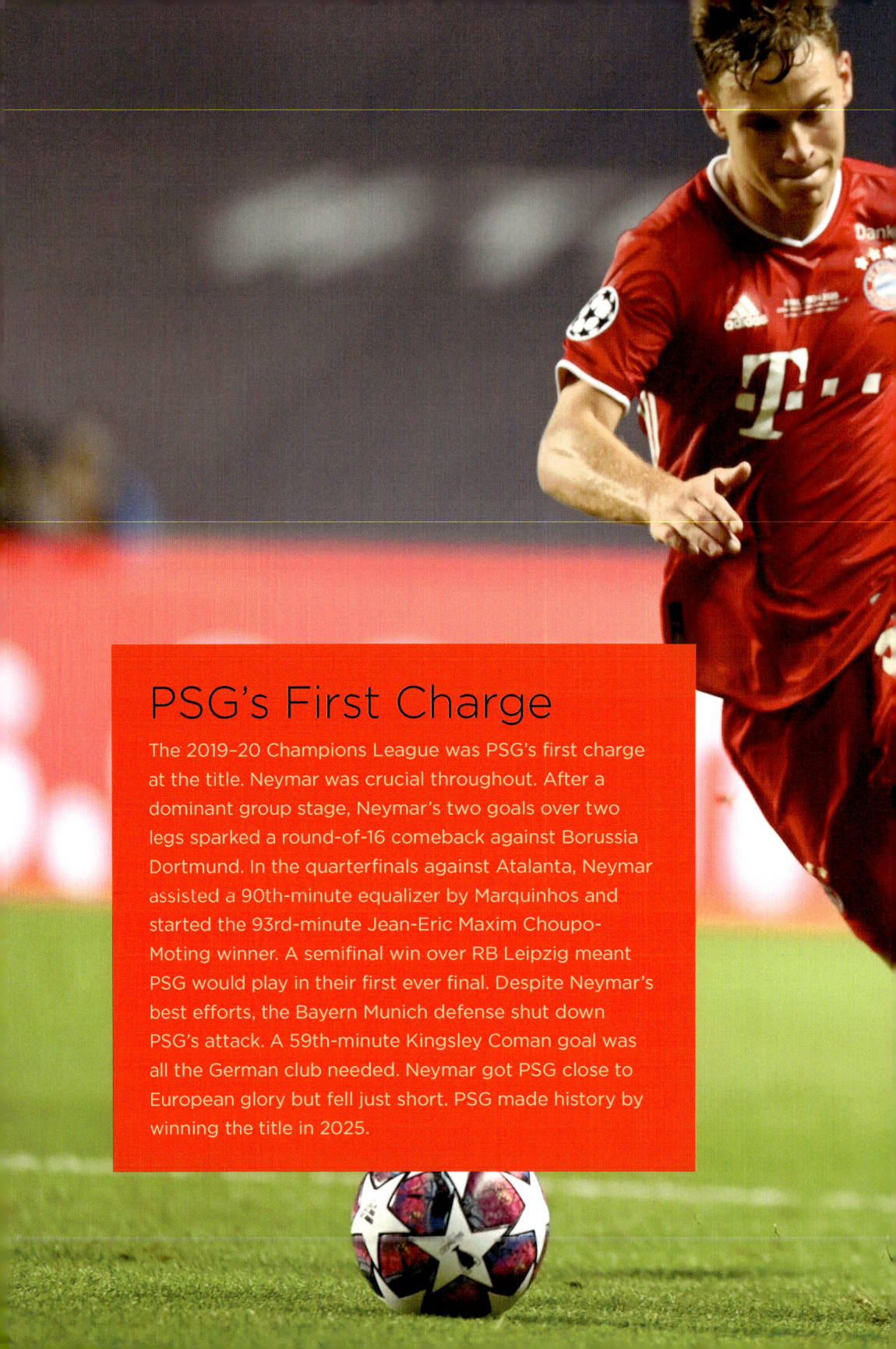

PSG's First Charge

The 2019–20 Champions League was PSG's first charge at the title. Neymar was crucial throughout. After a dominant group stage, Neymar's two goals over two legs sparked a round-of-16 comeback against Borussia Dortmund. In the quarterfinals against Atalanta, Neymar assisted a 90th-minute equalizer by Marquinhos and started the 93rd-minute Jean-Eric Maxim Choupo-Moting winner. A semifinal win over RB Leipzig meant PSG would play in their first ever final. Despite Neymar's best efforts, the Bayern Munich defense shut down PSG's attack. A 59th-minute Kingsley Coman goal was all the German club needed. Neymar got PSG close to European glory but fell just short. PSG made history by winning the title in 2025.

A Flopping Problem?

Neymar's 2018 World Cup performance was somewhat marred by a growing criticism of his on-field behavior. While he was a gifted player, Neymar was accused of flopping and making exaggerated reactions to fouls. This wasn't the first time, but it was the most prominent. Many saw this as a disgrace to the game, as using soccer's "dark arts" diminished his greatness. Fans, media members, and even opposing players weren't shy to call him out. The subject would not go away for the remainder of his career. Despite the controversy, Neymar was still one of the most entertaining players in the world.

where Neymar shined. Neymar drove PSG all the way to the Champions League final. Unfortunately for the Paris faithful, it was played in an empty stadium due to COVID restrictions. Furthermore, PSG lost 1–0 to Bayern Munich.

As Neymar entered his fourth season in Paris, fans hoped for a full season of appearances. Mbappé had turned into a superstar. Many started to believe this was his team, rather than Neymar's. Neymar eventually opened his 2020–21 account with a pair of goals against Angers in early October. But injury issues struck again, with an adductor issue forcing him to miss a month. Neymar's best performance of the season came in the Champions League group stage when he scored a hat trick against Turkish club İstanbul Başakşehir. His first goal was the pick of the bunch, as he **nutmegged** a

"PSG WEREN'T AS DOMINANT FOR THE FIRST TIME SINCE NEYMAR'S ARRIVAL."

defender to curl in a shot from outside the box. It made Neymar the first player ever to score 20 Champions League goals for two different clubs. But, two separate injuries soon forced him out for nearly two months. In his absence, PSG weren't as dominant for the first time since Neymar's arrival. Ultimately, they finished the Ligue 1 season second, a point behind Lille.

PSG were eager to try for another long Champions League run. Neymar had a fantastic quarterfinal, knocking out Bayern Munich. His two assists, in a torrential

Neymar reacts during a PSG game.

downpour, helped guide PSG into the semifinals. Against Manchester City, however, Neymar was shut down. The French club came up short yet again. Neymar ended the year with 17 goals in only 31 games, while Mbappé bore most of the scoring load. Still, Neymar committed to Paris, signing an extension until 2025.

NEYMAR

Injury Issues Mount

At the 2021 Copa América, Neymar was back in action for Brazil. He played well but again came up short, losing the final to Argentina. Seemingly out of nowhere, on August 10, PSG signed Neymar's former Barcelona teammate, Lionel Messi. PSG were building, on paper, one of the greatest attacking trios in history. A frontline of Messi, Mbappé, and Neymar was terrifying. But for

OPPOSITE: Neymar controls the ball during a 2021 Copa América match between Brazil and Colombia.

Neymar, more injury issues were the storyline, beginning with a November ankle injury. He missed nearly three months. This time, without Neymar, PSG were flying. Messi and Mbappé cruised through Ligue 1.

Neymar made his return in the first leg of a round-of-16 Champions League game with Real Madrid. Coming on as a substitute, Neymar assisted Mbappé's dramatic 94th-minute winner, to take the first leg 1–0. But things went sour in the second, as Real's Karim Benzema single-handedly knocked out the "dream team." PSG fans were critical of their club's performance considering the investment made with summer reinforcements. Neymar and teammates were even booed in league matches. Neymar played significant minutes in the season's latter half, but in mostly low-stakes games. He finished with 13 goals in 28 games, well behind Mbappé's 39. This

Mbappé and Neymar

2022 Qatar World Cup

marked Neymar's least-prolific season since arriving in Europe. Mbappé had become the face of PSG.

Once more, transfer rumors surrounded Neymar. But the price tag seemed too steep. While Neymar still had moments of breathtaking quality, they were just that, moments. Neymar got off to a flying start in the 2022–23 season. The star looked like the player of old, providing three assists and scoring in the opening Ligue 1 match of the year. Neymar scored twice more in the second game and had his best game of the season in a 7–1 thrashing of Lille. He scored twice and provided three assists. Through his first 20 games across all competitions, Neymar had scored 15 goals and assisted 11 more. He was in the best form of his Paris tenure. Then came the midseason 2022 Qatar World Cup. With Neymar on fire, many had Brazil as Cup favorites.

Neymar played well in the opener against Serbia, but, like so many times before, suffered ankle ligament damage. He was forced out of the remaining two group games. Brazil still advanced as group winners. In the round-of-16 match against South Korea, Neymar returned to assist Vinícius Júnior for the opener and score a penalty in a 4–1 win. Neymar joined Pelé and Ronaldo (Ronaldo Luís Nazário de Lima, unrelated to Cristiano Ronaldo) as the only Brazilians to score in three World Cups. In a nail-biting quarterfinal against Croatia, Neymar finished off an incredible team goal in extra time, gliding through the Croatian defense with a series of **1-2s**. But Croatia scored a shock equalizer. The game was sent to penalty kicks, and the Brazilians missed twice. Neymar, due fifth in the Brazilian order, never even had the chance to convert. The defeat was another sad World Cup moment for Neymar. His goal against Croatia was his 77th for the national team. It tied Pelé for most in a Brazil shirt. Pelé congratulated Neymar saying, "Keep inspiring us. I will keep punching the air with joy for every goal you score." Pelé died only weeks later. Equalizing the legend's tally was a remarkable achievement for Neymar.

Back with PSG, Neymar continued his stellar season. But a February ankle injury required major surgery, ending Neymar's season. His 18 goals in 29 games were impressive, but it was another abbreviated campaign.

Another failure in the Champions League led to more uproar from the fans. Some fans also demanded that Neymar leave. After two seasons, Messi announced he would leave PSG. On August 15, Neymar too, announced his departure from PSG. There were good and bad times in Paris for Neymar. He left the club scoring 118 career goals, fourth most all-time at PSG. He won 10 trophies with the club, but never the Champions League. Neymar missed an astonishing 119 matches for PSG from various injuries over his six years. The man who left Barcelona to step out of Messi's shadow had some masterful performances, only to once more be swallowed up by the shadow of Kylian Mbappé.

After six years in France, Neymar opted to follow several aging stars and take a lucrative transfer to Saudi Arabia with club Al-Hilal. His transfer fee was reported

Neymar's presence failed to gain PSG a Champions League trophy.

to be $98.6 million, which was the most expensive purchase in Saudi Pro League history. In September 2023, Neymar moved past Pelé's goal record, scoring twice in a 2026 World Cup qualifier against Bolivia. A week later, Neymar made his debut for Al-Hilal, assisting in the contest. He scored his first goal a few weeks later in an Asian Football Confederation Champions League group stage match. The competition level was a major step below the Spanish and French leagues, so expectations were for Neymar to dominate.

But in October, heartbreak struck, as Neymar was taken off in tears from a World Cup qualifier against Uruguay. It was another massive injury blow, as Neymar had ruptured his ACL and torn the meniscus in his left knee. He missed the rest of the 2023–24 season. Neymar only managed a few games for Al-Hilal in his debut season, scoring once and assisting three times. He attempted a comeback in November 2024 but was quickly sidelined with a hamstring tear. Neymar's big move to Saudi Arabia was going poorly for both player and club. He needed a fresh start.

On January 27, 2025, Al-Hilal announced the termination of Neymar's contract by mutual consent. It marked the end to a disappointing time in the desert, some calling it one of the worst transfers in soccer history. However, just three days later, Neymar announced he would rejoin his boyhood club Santos on a six-month contract. It was a beautiful, full-circle moment. Neymar returned to Brazilian league action on February 6 against Botafogo-SP. The fans gave their idol a raucous ovation. He was named captain and soon after scored his first goal since returning, converting a penalty against Água Santa.

A 2025 Santos match

In his first seven games with Santos, Neymar racked up three goals and three assists. The move brought new life to Neymar. He even hopes this stint in Brazil could rejuvenate a career in Europe.

All in all, Neymar has been one of the greatest players in the 21st century. It is undeniable that wherever he went, he made the club better. From his younger days in Santos, to his Champions League winning season with Barcelona and his numerous achievements with PSG, Neymar is a prolific, creative player. He also is one of the best ever to put on a Brazilian kit. However, the story of Neymar cannot be told without a sense of "what-if." What if Neymar hadn't gotten injured in the 2014 World Cup? What if Barcelona had kept Neymar with Messi and Suárez for years to come? What if Neymar had delivered a Champions League title to Paris? What if he had stayed healthy in key moments of his career and won a Ballon d'Or? Fair or not, these unanswered questions will always surround Neymar. Still, it is best to remember the highs and applaud his resilience; his ability to come back from the worst moments. One can hope Neymar will return to the dominant form he once had in the future, for both club and country.

Messi Takes the Glory Once More

The 2021 Copa América was Neymar's best chance to win a major international trophy. Brazil was dominant in the group stage, winning all three contests. Neymar had memorable moments in each, including assisting the 100th-minute winner from the corner against Colombia. Brazil squeaked past Chile and Peru with a pair of 1–0 wins, setting up a date with Argentina in the final. The game was again 1–0, but this time Argentina came out on top, with Neymar's PSG teammate Ángel Di María scoring the winner. Messi and Neymar embraced after the match, with Neymar's former teammate receiving the glory once more.

Selected Bibliography

Caioli, Luca. *Neymar: 2021 Updated Edition*. Icon Books, 2023.

Geoffreys, Clayton. *Neymar: The Inspiring Story of One of Soccer's Greatest Players*. Calavintir Books, 2023.

Goldblatt, David. *Futebol Nation: The Story of Brazil Through Soccer*. Bold Type Books, 2014.

"Neymar." *Encyclopedia Britannica*, 2024, https://www.britannica.com/biography/Neymar

"Neymar." *International Olympics Committee,* 2016, https://olympics.com/en/athletes/neymar -da-silva-santos-junior

Wilson, Jonathan. "How Neymar Has Come to Embody Soccer's Modern Age." *Sports Illustrated*, 2022, https://www.si.com/soccer/2022/02/04/neymar-30-career-expectations -brazil-world-cup-psg-champions-league

Glossary

1-2 a give-and-go pass

Ballon d'Or French for Golden Ball, soccer's most prestigious individual award

Campeonato Paulista
professional soccer league of São Paulo, Brazil

Champions League
annual competition featuring the top clubs across Europe, determining the best team in the continent

Confederations Cup
discontinued international tournament held the year before a World Cup with eight teams from across the world

Copa América South America's premier international tournament contested every four years

Copa do Brasil Brazil's premier single-elimination cup competition featuring club teams from across all regions

Copa Libertadores
annual competition featuring top clubs across South America, determining the best team in the continent

Coupe de France France's premier single-elimination cup competition featuring club teams from across all regions

Coupe de la Ligue
France's former secondary single-elimination cup competition that featured club teams from the top three leagues

El Clásico a match between Spanish clubs Barcelona and Real Madrid

FIFA stands for Fédération Internationale de Football Association (French), the governing body for soccer national teams and clubs around the world

friendly a non-competitive match without any impact on a league, tournament, or other event

futsal type of soccer player indoors on a hard surface. The field, ball, and team sizes are all smaller than traditional soccer.

La Liga top professional soccer league of Spain

Ligue 1 top professional soccer league of France

leg one of two matches between a pair of teams. Many soccer competitions use a two-legged system in their knockout phase.

nutmeg to dribble the ball through an opponent's legs and keep possession on the other side

Saudi Pro League
top professional soccer league of Saudi Arabia

transfer fee price paid by a soccer team to another to acquire a player who is under contract

treble   winning three major team trophies in a single season

UEFA   stands for Union of European Football Associations, the governing body for European national teams and clubs

Websites

Discover Neymar Jr's childhood in Brazil
www.redbull.com/us-en/discovering-neymar
A deep dive into Neymar's upbringing in Mogi das Cruzes

Football | Neymar Jr
www.neymarjr.com/en/football
Neymar's official website, filled with updates, videos, and news

Inside the Unstoppable Greatness of Neymar
mag.bleacherreport.com/neymar-brazil-world-cup-2018-larger-than-life/
A closer look at Neymar's impact on and off the field in Brazil

Neymar: The Perfect Chaos
www.netflix.com/title/81005126
Netflix's three-part docuseries that focuses on the highs and lows throughout Neymar's career

Index

academy, 14, 20
assists, 21, 27, 30, 32, 33, 37, 38, 41, 45, 47, 54, 58, 62, 65, 66, 70, 71, 73, 75
awards
   Ballon d'Or, 36, 45, 74
   Ligue 1 Player of the Year, 47
   Man of the Match, 31
   UEFA Team of the Year, 33
captain, 36, 71
competitions
   Campeonato Paulista, 15, 21
   Champions League, 36, 39, 41, 45, 46, 49, 51, 53, 54, 57, 58, 62, 68, 70, 73, 74
   Club World Cup, 26, 37
   Copa América, 36, 52, 61, 75
   Copa do Brasil, 17, 25
   Copa Libertadores, 18
   Confederations Cup, 24, 27, 31
   Coupe de France, 53
   Olympics, 38, 40, 46
   World Cup, 9, 17, 27, 31, 32, 47, 56, 65, 66, 70, 74
contracts, 20, 41, 42, 71
controversy
   flopping, 56
   red card, 36–37
   social media, 52
creativity, 20, 30, 73
debuts, 14, 17, 29, 44, 47, 70, 71
El Clásico, 30
fans, 10, 18, 20, 22, 23, 25, 27, 38, 44, 45, 56, 57, 62, 68, 71
father, 13
free kicks, 40, 41, 43, 49
futsal, 13
group stage, 18, 21, 31, 54, 57, 70, 75
injury
   ACL, 70
   adductor, 57
   ankle, 62, 66, 67
   foot, 47, 48, 51
knockout stage, 18, 21, 38, 39

La Remontada, 49
leadership, 41
MSN, 32, 36, 37, 38
Pelé, 10, 14, 18, 21, 66, 67, 70
Ronaldinho, 23
Ronaldo, 66
Ronaldo, Cristiano, 10, 45, 66
rumors, 42, 52, 65
South America, 17, 26
stadium, 9, 25, 32, 43, 57
teammates
   Cavani, Edinson, 44
   Di María, Ángel, 44
   Mbappé, Kylian, 44, 57, 59, 61, 62, 63, 65, 68
   Messi, Lionel, 10, 25, 30, 31, 32, 33, 38, 41, 42, 44, 45, 61, 62, 68, 74
   Sánchez, Alexis, 30
   Suárez, Luis, 32, 37, 38, 41, 44, 74
teams
   Al-Hilal, 68, 70, 71
   Barcelona, 23, 25, 27, 29, 30, 32, 33, 34, 36, 37, 39, 41, 42, 44, 47, 49, 52, 68, 73, 74
   Brazil national team, 9, 10, 26, 27, 31, 32, 36, 38, 40, 43, 48, 51, 61, 65, 66, 67, 75
   Paris Saint-Germain, 39, 41, 42, 45, 47, 51–54, 57–62, 65, 67, 73, 75
   Santos, 13, 14, 15, 17, 18, 20, 21, 22, 23, 25, 26, 37, 71, 72, 73
trophy, 37, 75
transfer, 25, 42, 44, 47, 65, 68, 71
youth, 14, 20